Contents

one

Four years back, a special little woman was birthed at 12:01 on Christmas day-- the very first infant arrival of Xmas that year.

Her mommy called her Siobhan (noticable sha-vawn) after the finest close friend she had when she lived in Ireland. It was the initial name that came to her mind when she held her little girl in her arms.

Being the first youngster born on Christmas wasn't specifically the same as being the first born on New Year's, with the infant obtaining prizes as well as gifts. A Christmas wonder dream.

" Do not think it? Well, I existed." "I existed also."

" Well, I was the one that gave her the very first dream." "As well as I offered her the 2nd."

" We did it at the same time. "And also therefore the reason why you require me. Allow's not transform this right into a tiff."

" Forgive me, proceed."

" Now, I know you're wondering who we are. Contrary to what you might hear, we do not look like little fairies."

" That's. Christmas angels are not fairies." "You used the A word. You weren't supposed to." "Move on with the tale, please."

Visualize a day in late December, just a couple of days before Christmas.

In a park at the center of the city, youngsters smile vibrantly, seeing the miniature red train slow so they can have their rely on ride.

Holiday lights and also decors cover the home windows of every store front bordering the park. Snow motifs in shades of blue and also white drape in an arc from one side of the road to the other. Rotating red-and-white sweet poinsettias, angels, and walking sticks made from garland and lights, decorate the lamp articles.

Crystal City is like most hectic cities this time of year. Every person is specifically nice, claiming hello or excuse me when passing, drinking warm drinks as they walk with their noses red from the cold.

They remain in a rush to get home. There is dinner to be made, presents to cover, and also areas to get ready for loved ones.

This isn't a story regarding them. It's a tale concerning the young boy racing by with his knapsack. A wool cap covers his freshly-cut burst-fade reduced mohawk. He 'd stopped at the barber to make sure he looked good for Christmas.

School is out for wintertime break, as well as he just left Rowland's Pawnshop. His ideal friend, Mikey, informed him it was the best location to discover all kinds of Christmas presents.

Moments ago inside the store, Mikey tapped the glass, leaving a spot on the case. "What about this?"

" Sir, just how much is that?" asked Jared.

" Hang on a minute, fellas." The staff's hand raked via his hair, unnaturally black for his age, as he pointed out something on a woman's watch.

Jared leaned back against the jewelry case, scanning the rows of musical tools, tvs, and also laptop computers. "Mikey, what are chestnuts?"

He quit banging a beat out with his wrist on the glass and laughed. "Why would you ask that?"

" The tune that's playing. Chestnuts toasting on an open fire?" "That's not the name of the tune. It's The Christmas Song." "Well, since you know the title, what are they?"

Mikey eliminated the hood of his orange extra-large sweatshirt, uncovering his dark curly hair. He constantly used huge shirts to hide the dimension of his belly. , if he just knew every person could still see it.

." Just how the heck would I know? Do you see city children around right

here with chestnuts?
" Duh, ya believe?" Jared replied.
The salesperson thanked a consumer for being available in and also strolled to the children. "What can I provide for you gentlemen?"
" How much is that locket?" asked Jared.
The clerk pointed to a giant cross on a thick gold chain inside the jewelry case. "This?"
Jared directed and frowned to the pendant next to it. "Not that. The one to the right. No, the other way."
" Oh, you imply my other right," the staff stated with a laugh. He took the pendant out of the situation and also carefully laid it on a red velvet fabric on the
You have good taste. That's genuine gold-plated silver."
Jared and also Mikey relocated more detailed, admiring it. They both responded. "That's the one," Jared said.
" That's a dove there on the pendant. For somebody special, huh?" "Yep.". The clerk elevated an eyebrow. "For your girly?" "She's a lady but not my girly.".
" I'll inform you what." The clerk damaged his chin. "I like you, and also I do not like many people. I'm going to allow you have it at a swipe.".
" Regardless of just how much he states, go lower," Mikey murmured.
" I got this," Jared whispered back. "What do you think about a steal? I don't have a great deal of money. I'm just eleven.".
" Eleven you claim? I would certainly've assumed you were at least eleven and also a fifty percent.
Just how much do you have?".
Jared smirked. He unzipped his coat and took out his pocketbook, which was a birthday gift from his mom previously that year. A penny spun until Mikey put it down with his palm.
" Well, what do you recognize? The staff winked at Mikey and looked over at the woman assisting an additional consumer.
" I'll take it," said Jared. "Cover that up for me, and I'll include a--" he looked his other pocket. "A round of dust.".
" You're dumb." Mikey claimed with a laugh while shoving him.
Outside the shop with his brand-new acquisition, Jared interlaced his thumb with.

Mikey's, and they wiggled their fingers. "Many thanks, man. I owe you one.".

Mikey drew his hand back and they both broke their fingers. You told him exactly just how much you had. Why really did not you use ten dollars?

" I got what I came for, didn't I? So stop nagging.".

Mikey lifted the hood of his sweatshirt over his head as well as zoomed his coat. "I'm simply saying. Anyhow, we would certainly better hurry prior to we're grounded, and also our gifts are hidden away till following Christmas.".

Jared laughed. "Your parents are serious. I neglected they did that to you."

The kids ran down several blocks till Mikey quit, out of breath,.

as well as held on to a parking meter. "Can you decrease?".

" You're the one that wanted to rush. Do you want to enter problem for going midtown without an adult?".

" A minimum of we went together," Mikey responded as he trudged along after him.

It was an advantage they didn't live far. But they still had to cross over a pedestrian bridge before arriving at the main road that led to their neighborhood.

" Hey!" a man screamed from an auto.

" Stranger risk," Mikey mumbled as he as well as Jared took their mobile phone from their coat pockets and also held them up.

" Live streaming," Jared screamed. "This scary individual in this car is--"

The auto sped off, as well as they continued recording until it ran out view.

Mikey tapped on his screen. "Were you fast enough this moment? Did you get it?".

" Yep. Sending it to my mommy today so she can publish and also share it or tag the cops or whatever she does.".

" Crystal City PD ought to put our mamas on pay-roll.".

" I recognize, best?".

The kids made it to Mikey's street equally as snow flurries started to drop. Jared aimed at him as he walked backward. "My home, Christmas Eve. Do not fail to remember. See ya.".

" When have I ever before missed out on Xmas Eve dinner?".

" Attempt not to consume too much before after that. You're already

breaking out of your clothing!".
Mikey attempted and stooped to make a snowball, however the snow was also light as well as fine-grained. "Ah, neglect it," he stated as he combed the snow from his hands. "You got lucky this moment.".
Jared had actually prepared to dodge it yet chuckled and also jogged away.
He hurried to his apartment over the freshly-salted sidewalks, humming The Xmas Song and beaming with satisfaction. His mom would receive the first Christmas gift that she really did not give him the money to acquire. Typically, she would certainly take him buying as well as give him a couple of bucks to pick something out-- with her waiting at the end of the aisle, acting like she couldn't see it. This moment, he would certainly saved his lunch money to stun her.
Jared would need to find out a great place to hide the necklace from his little sis.
Snicker got involved in everything, since she could stroll. He would certainly located her standing on the rail of her baby crib, reaching up into the storage room as soon as when she was a little over one year old.
" Mother, Snicker's doing it again!" he would certainly yelled while ordering her around the waistline to bring her down.
His mommy called his little sibling Snickerdoodle, however Jared reduced it to Snicker. Never Jared, however Bro. Especially when she saw him coming house from college and was so excited.
Jared added to his apartment building with his type in hand. Somebody was appearing and also held the door open for him.
" Merry Christmas," the man stated in passing.
" Merry Christmas," Jared shouted behind him as he ran through the entrance hall and also up the stairways to his flooring.
Trixie added to him as quickly as he entered the corridor.
" You insane pet cat. Just how do you maintain going out?" He grabbed his grey feline as well as slowed as he came close to the house. The door was open.
A month back, that house had actually been burglarized. Jared didn't know if his television had actually been also loud or if he would certainly been putting on earphones, yet they would certainly been simply throughout the hall and he would certainly never ever listened to an audio. The thieves

could have come back and targeted his apartment or condo next.
His heart defeated fast. His family had nothing a burglar would want. They weren't abundant, and there had not been anything under their tree to take. His mom always placed their gifts on layaway, after that got them out on Christmas Eve as well as spent all night covering them. Although, she told them the gifts were left by angels-- not Santa, however angels. He had actually visualized a lot of small angels that looked like Tinker Bell when he was younger. He 'd imagined them glowing and flying right into their apartment or condo, lugging gifts together and lowering them in front of the tree.
But he would certainly understood the fact. He saw his mom when, tiptoeing out of her bed room in the middle of the evening. She 'd held a pile of presents, some covered in red covering paper with snowmen and others in silver glitter and glossy blue paper. Lights had flickered on the wall down the hall from the Xmas tree as he would certainly seen his mom's darkness in the living room.
He had after that searched in her room and seen a lot more boxes on her bed, in addition to bow, tape, and also scissors. The floor had actually creaked, and also he would certainly rushed back to his area and also hopped in his bed before she might catch him. He 'd then faced the wall surface and breathed greatly, attempting to show up asleep, and also really did not let down in revealing shock and joy at seeing the presents under the tree the following morning.
Currently, no noises came from the various other apartment or condos on the flooring. With each slow-moving action Jared took toward the door, his legs came to be harder to move.
A shrill wail originated from Trixie. He should have been pressing her. She agonized and leapt from his arms.
Jared stopped right outside the house, looking in, not seeing any kind of movement. He put his hand level versus the door listed below the wreath and gradually pressed it open. Red, yellow, and environment-friendly clouds of light reviewed the opposite wall surface from their small fabricated tree.
His eyes expanded. In a quick movement, he leapt back, knocking himself versus the opposite wall surface.
" Mother!" Jared yelled as he slid to the floor

two

A person's feet lay face-down on the flooring across from Jared. Immediate screeches escape from him. His sobs go back and forth between "Mommy" and "Help.".

" Jared, what's wrong?" asked his next-door neighbor, Mrs. Hollis, racing down the hall from the lift.

" I heard you prior to the elevator doors opened up." She stooped and also put her bags on the floor. "Jared, what took place, child?".

He wept right into her shoulder. She hugged him tightly and turned, checking out the apartment or condo.

" Oh, no!" she said loudly as she started to stand.

" No! Do not go in there," stated Jared, drawing her back.

" It's all right. I'll remain right where you can see me. Will that work?" He sniffed and nodded.

" Wait here," she claimed, after that pushed the home door all the way open as well as stepped inside.

Jared watched her as she stooped over his mommy's body, looking for a pulse. Her hands trembled as she took her phone from the bag that hung at her waist. She reversed to him as well as place the telephone call on audio speaker.

" 911, what is your emergency situation?" asked the driver.

" I need to report ..." She glanced at Jared. "A crash.".

Cops police officers and also paramedics made the small living-room really feel also smaller. They 'd relocated the coffee table as well as overturned the tiny Christmas tree. A gold glass light bulb shattered on the floor and ground under an officer's foot.

Jared as well as Mikey moved more detailed, admiring it. "That's the one," Jared claimed.

" I obtained this," Jared whispered back." I'll take it," said Jared. Jared quit right outside the apartment, looking in, not seeing any type of movement.

Neighbors stood in the hall around the door, watching what was going on within and also standing up phones. They maintained having to be asked to return.

Jared rested on the sofa with his hand up, securing his face from the sight of where his mom lay.

" What are you doing?" asked one of the policemans. "Obtain him out of right here.

Don't allow him see her like that."

A paramedic drew a sheet over her face. "We're waiting on the medical supervisor."

It had not been that Jared didn't want to look at his mommy. He intended to remember her the way he had actually seen her that early morning before he left for school. The way she grinned at him as she put batter on the waffle iron and bit his item of bacon off before he can get it to his mouth. The way she listened intently to his story about Mikey attempting to rip off on his examination. Her embrace, lifting him from the floor, before he left. The scent of the shea butter on her skin. Exactly how could he have recognized it was the last hug he 'd ever before receive? He would've embraced her harder, longer.

" It appears like she was preparing to leave. One arm was in her layer," an officer kept in mind.

Jared jumped from the sofa. "Where is my sibling?"

" What sis? He has a sister?" the police officer asked, taking a look around the living room. He snatched a little picture frame from the shelf and also held it up for the other police officer to see.

Mrs. Hollis held Jared. The officer looked at her.

" No, I'm his neighbor. The one who called. The other policeman already took my declaration."

" Do you recognize his family members-- a person we can find?"

" I'm sorry, I don't." Mrs. Hollis considered Jared. "Jared, do you have household in the area or anywhere nearby?" she asked. "I do not think your mother ever before pointed out any individual to me."

He trembled his head.

Another police officer crossed the area as well as decreased his voice. "The Department of Kid and Family members is working out positioning for him."

" He states he has a sibling," a policeman murmured. "Where is she?"

Mrs. Hollis browsed the living room. "His mom's phone is right there. Maybe there's a number. Jared, do you know the passcode?"

"Take me to my sister."

Jared rode in the backseat of a black car that you would never recognize was a police car. There were no lights on the top or markings to distinguish it from any

other Dodge Battery charger.

He really felt numb as they passed the many homes with home windows framed in multi-colored lights for Christmas. They no longer caught his interest. Nor did the gigantic Santa and reindeer inflatables on the lawns. It didn't suggest anything to him any longer. As for he was concerned, everything outside the window was a film-- all the happiness, all the laughter. It was all phony. The pain and also hurt he felt was the real life.

The ride was the lengthiest it had actually ever taken to reach Ms. Merna's residence. She dealt with a lot of the younger youngsters in your area and had the regard of every person in the community. All the youngsters stood out at reading as a result of her, including Jared.

Jared did as soon as when he didn't wear a belt. Ms. Merna observed his trousers drooping as well as went to obtain her button.

She always intimidated youngsters with the thin branch with fallen leaves carried out, however her fussing was enough to align any person out.

Jared sniffed and also massaged his eyes. At this time of the night, Ms. Merna would be preparing supper-- something Caribbean. He imagined Snicker, her body clock telling her it was almost time to go. She 'd put on her layer prior to being asked to do so. She would certainly stand in the window, enjoying each automobile that drove by as well as waiting for their mommy to select her up.

How do you tell a three-year-old that her mother is gone? It looked like simply the other day Snicker was drinking from a container. Mommy was her whole globe. If I hadn't mosted likely to that stupid pawnshop, I would've existed. I could have helped her.

three

He grimaced, obviously irritated. Every time he tried to exit the lobby, the superintendent started speaking again.

He held a device belt in one hand as well as eliminated his various other hand from his grey coveralls to direct around the door. "I have actually informed you in the past, do not have your packages left at the door. That resembles saying, 'Hey, I ordered something. Select it up and also take it house.' They have lockers they'll deliver them to."

Jared glanced at them as he strolled by and also pulled his hood over his head, protecting his face. He turned along the side of the structure as well as looked up at the fire escape. There was a parking lot below it. He climbed onto its trunk and also up on the dumpster behind it.

It took him a number of dives to pull down the emergency exit. The steel was cold as well as grew cooler with each understanding of a called. He reached each floor with a grocery bag hanging from his arm, praying it would not damage.

Eight trips up, Jared arrived at his living room window. It was cracked open, just as he 'd left it. He pushed it up, pressed back the curtains, as well as climbed inside, attempting to tip over the couch cushions.

The apartment was the exact same as he would certainly left it. The deadbolts were secured, as well as Snicker was still snoozing. He had no option however to leave her alone.

Besides the light from the refrigerator, the house was dark. The drapes were drawn, and they attempted not to utilize the electricity-- except when Snicker went to the bathroom. Jared didn't recognize what monster she had actually seen in there, but she refused to do without light.

He counted on the table and also put the soggy remnants of Snicker's early morning dish of cereal in the sink. There were two things they ate, due to the fact that there were only two things he recognized how to make: grain

and peanut butter and jelly sandwiches.
Snicker would stir up quickly for her sandwich and also milk, and after that invest the afternoon begging for a trip to the park.
Jared swiftly spread out peanut butter over a piece of bread and also slathered it with grape jelly.
A pounding at the door created his heart to race. By the means whoever it was knocked, there was no opportunity the person would go away.
He tiptoed to the door and listened.
A man's voice originated from the other side. "Did he go to institution?"
"They're still on break," another voice replied.
Jared blew out a breath and checked out the area. Snicker strolled right into the living room wearing pants, a sweatshirt, as well as a tutu. She massaged her eyes as she always did for almost a half hr, up until she was fully awake.
An additional pound slammed on the door.
" Jared, child, we know you're in there."
Jared hadn't removed his coat or hat yet. He held his finger to his mouth, his eyes begging with Snicker not to say anything. Yet that simply wasn't her. She talked a lot as well as was loud. To his shock, this time around she paid attention. She remained silent as he put her arms in her layer as well as pulled her hat over her curly, poofy braid. He took her to the couch as well as climbed out of the window. "What about Trixie?" she asked, really whispering for when. The grey cat appeared on the windowsill.
" She'll be fine until we come back. There's a sandwich on the table."
They climbed out onto the emergency exit, and also Jared lowered the window, leaving it split open.
Snicker started to descend the ladder, and Jared climbed up over her, ensuring she got hold of hold and her foot arrived at each rung. At the

bottom, he leapt from the dumpster and also Snicker jumped into his arms with a laugh. It was all a video game to her, and also he rejoiced. Finding another home for them was not going to be very easy. Soon enough, the police would certainly kick in the door of the apartment. And when they opened up the door, they would certainly discover all the parcels Jared had actually taken that had been left at the main door.

" Get on, Snicker." Jared claimed as he stooped. She climbed onto his back, as well as he rushed throughout of the alley.

" Hold it right there," claimed the police officer that stepped in front of him. Jared spun around to go the various other way, assuming he could elude the male.

Another police officer walked up from behind him. He breathed out difficult and stared at the ground.

" Allow's go, Jared," said the very first officer. He spoke right into his shoulder mic. "We have a 7001."

" What does that imply?" Jared asked as he strolled together with them. "Runaway recuperated."

four

Jared feared wintertime as a result of nights such as this, with Snicker hugged versus his side, shivering.

" It's chilly, Brother."

He drew the strings of her hood, tightening it around her face, and raised her scarf over her nose as well as mouth. "I understand, Snicker.

" I desire Mommy." "Bear in mind, Mommy is gone."

" Her heart stopped working," Snicker responded, looking up at Jared with doe eyes.

" That's right."

" She remains in paradise with the stars." Snicker coughed and cleaned her nose with her gloved hand. "I'm going to pick which celebrity is her," she claimed, seeking out at the skies.

" Yes, allow's do that." Jared would certainly do anything to maintain Snicker's mind off the chilly as well as their circumstance.

They didn't stick out in the open where everyone can see, or a person might call the police or take them away. When they listened to an auto drive up, they were stooping next to a trash container glancing from the side of a paired house.

" There's one! I hear it," Snicker stated.

Jared looked out at the aesthetic. Snicker was right. A man got out of the motorist's side of an SUV and also took an overnight bag out of the trunk before going inside the building.

Jared gradually stepped off the pathway and stood behind the auto. He held his arms out toward his sis.

Snicker scooted over to him, and also Jared smiled down at her. The heat placed a smile on both of their faces, and Jared drew his sis in close to him.

She slept almost quickly.

" It will not constantly be like this, Snickerdoodle," he whispered. "Do you hear?".

" Yes," she mumbled.

Many nights he told her tales up until she fell asleep. In some cases he made them up. Other times they had to do with their mommy before she went to heaven as well as how much she enjoyed them.

Tonight he was also weary. And as he felt his fingers thawing, he only said, "Snicker, remember the park.".

A canine barked on the sidewalk as well as sniffed around the visual. Behind them, an automobile door pounded. Jared's eyes flashed open. He would certainly sleep in. He felt close to him and looked to his. Snicker was gone. The auto behind the SUV supported and also retreated. Jared rapidly presented from under the automobile, rigid and chilly. He recognized better than to stay in the air like that all night.

Snicker could not have obtained much, however there were no signs of her impacts. What if she's been taken by the cops or a complete stranger?

This had not been the very first time Snicker disappeared. She strayed virtually each day. She was 4 years old as well as enjoyed to discover. Not just that, but Snicker loved people as well as trusted everybody.

Jared ran back to their apartment building as well as climbed up the fire escape, thinking maybe she would certainly gone house. The window was closed and also locked. He cupped his hand versus it and peered within.

New curtains mounted the home window, as well as the walls were painted white-- as opposed to the old shade that advised him of rushed eggs. Their brown sofa had actually been changed with a grey sectional, and also there was a large television installed on the wall.

It didn't feel like he would certainly ever lived there. Somebody had actually removed everything that advised him of his mother. It left a lump in his throat. He glanced at the white Christmas tree with pink and gold light bulbs and backed.

away.

Downy snow trembled to the ground and promptly thawed over the shoveled and salted drive. Jared strolled with his head down and also as he turned the corner, a leopard patterned layer ran smack right into his face.

A shrill voice welcomed him. "Jared? Is that you? What are you doing below?".

" Mrs. Hollis, hi. Have you seen my sibling?".

" No honey, not since--" She removed her throat. "It's been nearly a year, hasn't it? Exactly how are you?".

Jared searched for the block. "Fine.".

" What regarding your foster home? Are they treating you well? It must neighbor, huh?".

" I'm searching for my sister," Jared responded.

" I have not seen her, honey." She examined him and cleaned the dust spot from the side of his face. "Walk with me, will you?".

Jared began to state something, but then quit. He tipped and also responded along with her.

" I choose coffee and also a croissant every early morning. When it's cold-- till there's too much snow and ice, even. It's good for my legs.".

She turned into a little coffee shop at the end of the following block. Jared coughed and drew his hat listed below his ears. "I'll see you--".

" Be available in and also have something," Mrs. Hollis claimed while holding the door open.

" I don't have any kind of cash.".

" It's my treat. I'm inviting you." "Uh, alright.".

He rested at a booth paying attention to Bossa Nova Christmas songs. His hands and feet tingled as they began to thaw.

Mrs. Hollis removed her layer as well as set it unemployed close to her as Jared clasped his hands with each other in his lap as well as leaned back, wishing she could not scent that he hadn't cleaned his teeth-- in days.

The waitress came close to, pushing back her slouch hat, and after that wiped her hands on her apron.

Jared really did not understand what beast she had actually seen in there, yet she declined to go without light.

Snicker began to come down the ladder, as well as Jared climbed up over her, making sure she grabbed hold and her foot landed on each sounded." Allow's go, Jared," said the initial officer. Snicker scampered over to him, and Jared smiled down at her. Jared ran back to their house building and also climbed the fire retreat, thinking perhaps she 'd gone home.

"What would certainly you such as?" Mrs. Hollis asked as she looked up at the menu covering the whole wall behind the counter.

" I do not know," said Jared. "He'll have a hot delicious chocolate?" Jared nodded.

The waitress paid attention without writing anything down.

" As well as among those morning meal sandwiches. You know, Sebi's specialty. And also you currently recognize what I obtain."

" Are you sure you do not want to change it up today? We have a great frittata."

" Thank you, honey, but my stomach might challenge it in the worst method."
"Obtained it," the waitress responded with a laugh.
Mrs. Hollis turned her attention to Jared. "You can've tried one of the holiday beverages if you desired. Eggnog--".
" That respects holiday stuff?".
She relocated closer to the table as well as stretched her neck toward him. "Holiday stuff? Do not give up on Christmas right now.".
" What's that intended to suggest?".
" I have actually heard inform of angels that supervise youngsters. Specifically around this time of year.".
" As well as what takes place?".
Her eyes became intense as she positioned her hands level on the table as well as leaned in as for she could. "Miracles." She pressed off her hands and also straightened.
with a smile.
Jared increased his brow. "You're making that up.".
" No, I'm not. My granny told me years ago concerning Xmas angels that give dreams. I have actually simply never had youngsters of my very own to share the tale with, so I'm mosting likely to share it with you.".
" Right here you are," claimed the waitress, plunking their food on the table.
Jared looked at the bacon, egg, and also cheese on Texas toast. "This is for me?".
Mrs. Hollis responded. "You're young, you need much more calories than an old female.".
" Are you certain?" "Go on, eat.".
Jared began with a sip of hot chocolate. The warmth of it streamed to his upper body and also tummy and emitted external. An ah noise may have escaped him without him understanding it, but Mrs. Hollis didn't eye him or

reveal any indicator she observed.

" What were you stating about the angels?" he asked.

Mrs. Hollis took a bite of her croissant as well as offered a green light to the person behind the counter. "Your sis was born on Xmas, had not been she?" she asked.

" Yes.".

" After that she is really unique. She obtains a dual true blessing in the type of a desire.

One amazing miracle each year. Yet ...".

Jared couldn't take his eyes off her. "However what?".

" She only has till dusk on Xmas to make the wish." "Any type of type of wish?".

" It's Xmas. The wish should show love as well as selflessness. Eat. Your food is obtaining cold.".

Mrs. Hollis saw him meticulously take half the sandwich, wrap it in a.

napkin, as well as place it in his pocket. "What are you doing?".

He took a huge bite of the various other fifty percent. "Conserving fifty percent for Snicker. She'll be starving when I discover her." He stopped briefly for a moment. "I bet you're mosting likely to tell me there's a bad beast that will stop the wish from taking place.".

" No. Just you.".

" Me?".

Mrs. Hollis giggled. "Not you. I imply individuals as a whole. Their unbelief in wonders. Their absence of hope." She included five sugars to her coffee as well as mixed. "Do you count on miracles?".

" Maybe.".

" Where do you think Siobhan is?" "At the park. She loves the park.".

" She's also young to venture out to the park alone and also in this climate.

Are you sure?".

Jared coughed as well as turned right into his elbow joint. He leaned back on the cubicle seat and also took a look around the cafe before taking an additional bite of his half-sandwich.

Mrs. Hollis watched him. "Jared, honey, are you okay? You don't look well.".

He ran across the bench as well as stood. "I'm great. I require to go." He gulped down the hot delicious chocolate, which was now amazing. "She'll be trying to find me, and if I do not show--" Jared resorted to the door as well as recalled. "Many thanks for morning meal. It was nice to see you once more." He stared at the floor a minute, bearing in mind the last time he 'd seen Mrs. Hollis. "And thank you for the tale.".

" It's not just a story, Jared.".

" Okay." He lifted his hand, saying goodbye, and also pushed the door open with his shoulder.

Jared ran completely to the park. It was early, so there was no one around,.

with the exception of the guys setting up the live Christmas trees available for sale. He walked the entire park, and then sat staring in advance at an Italian restaurant across the street with phony snow sprayed on the windows.

" Simply hear those sleigh bells ding ..." piped from the speakers outside of the plaza.

I have to locate her. I just have until Xmas. Afterwards, I'll need to wait an entire nother year. As well as if they catch me again, they're mosting likely to ensure I can not escape the next time. Snicker, where are you?

five

" Luca, garbage.".

He brushed his lengthy composes of his face and also looked up at his daddy. "Pop, I'm busing tables. That's Tony's task.".

His father popped him on the back of the head. "I uncommitted that does it as long as it obtains done.".

Tony giggled, claiming to be active counting invoices.

Luca dropped the tray and whined on the counter-- hard, so everyone would certainly listen to the glasses and plates smashing and know just how dismayed he was. Tony was fifteen, 2 years older than him, and Luca figured he was their daddy's favorite. He escaped every little thing.

Luca knocked his clenched fist on the swinging door, strolled to the area beyond the storeroom, as well as ordered the two trash can that were waiting. He thought he had the worse life of any type of teenager, and that all his papa wanted from him was work. He took a progression, and his apron got on the door, yanking him in reverse.

" Fantastic! Just terrific!" he groaned and kicked one of the bags. After that he pulled his apron away and utilized his back to press open the back door of the restaurant.

He tipped outside, shuddering in the fragile air with a trash can in each.

hand like he was a range of justice. He turned toward the dumpster.

" I despise this location," he mumbled as he observed activity to the left of him.

A kid quit-- mid-scoot-- from under the firm vehicle. They looked dewy-eyed at each various other, neither of them saying a thing.

The boy looked like he 'd been crying. Luca looked up and down the alley.

" Luca, what are you doing?" His papa asked from the door. "Why aren't these bags in the dumpster?".

" Pop, quit micromanaging. I got it. "With no coat on?

the lunch rush begins," he claimed and returned within.

Luca chose up the bags and threw them in the dumpster. He looked back at the place where the child had actually lain.

That night was the first time Luca ever had insomnia. He transformed as well as threw, considering the young boy. "What was he doing under the truck?".

The child had been unclean and frail looking. As well as terrified.

Luca sat up in bed. He leapt up and also went down to the cooking area.

" What are you reconstructing?" Luca asked.

" Looking at these spreadsheets. What concerning you?".

" Pop, uh, I was wondering ... Have you ever before seen a homeless child?".

" In Crystal City? Why, have you seen a homeless child?".

" I do not recognize.".

" Well, if you do, call the police officers and also get him off the roads. That's no life for.

a youngster.".

The next early morning before going to the dining establishment, Luca packed a bag of toothpaste, food and tooth brush, a pair of socks, hand warmers, as well as wipes from the restaurant. He added a note.

Are you homeless?

Call this number if you require anything. They will help you.

I have something that belongs to you. Luca.

About the same time as the day in the past, he went outside and searched for the kid. The vehicle had not been there due to the fact that there were no shipment, and also neither was the kid. He established the bag on top of a couple of empty cages.

Anytime he could flee, he examined the alley. The bag was still there.

The following day, he did the exact same. When he went out the back entrance to examine the bag, the young boy was there, holding the bag and looking prepared to run.

I'm not going to do anything to you. Luca slowly strolled toward him with his hands up. Just nod.".

" I can talk," the kids said. "I simply didn't intend to. Did you-- are you the one who left this for me?".

He waited however didn't get an action. I'll inform you what, come within as well as clean up and use the things I place in that bag. Later, I'll obtain you a warm plate.".

The young boy looked perplexed. "To stick in my layer?".

" No. Sheesh, the length of time have you been out here? To eat-- I indicate, with food on it to consume.".

" For real?" "Yes.".

" Okay.".

" Follow me." Luca maintained evaluating his shoulder to see to it the boy had not vanished. He pushed the door open. "Right in there.".

" Many thanks." The young boy stepped within. "Stop with all the smiling-- looking all proud of on your own.".

Luca led him to the toilet, and the young boy went in. The door slowly shut behind him, and after that the child seized open. "Are you going to stand there the whole time?".

" Oh, no. I indicate, I had not been trying to-- I'll be right over there." Luca transferred to the eating hall to give him some privacy.

5 mins later on, Luca saw him leave the bathroom and get in the eating hall with his coat over his arm. "Wow, look at you. I didn't recognize what color of brownish you were until now.".

The young boy tightened his eyes at him. "Why are you talking like we're friends?".

" Due to the fact that we are.".

" As well as why doesn't your bathroom have a mirror?" "My brother's face broke it.".

The kid most likely didn't want Luca to observe, but he nearly laughed.

" Sit down, buddy," stated Luca, gesturing to the tables. "I'll go and obtain your plate.".

" Anywhere?".

" Yeah, the dining establishment's empty. Simply don't leave.".

Luca backed right into the cooking area, as well as the cook handed him a plate. "Great.

Many thanks, Antony.".

He rushed back to the dining room and set the plate of pasta as well as garlic bread before the young boy. "Be careful, home plate is warm," Luca stated as he rested throughout from him.

The young boy dug his fork into the lasagna and also lifted the bite to his mouth. Cheese pulled from the plate to his fork. His eyes curtailed as he chewed.

" Great, huh?" asked Luca. He nodded.

After he would certainly taken a number of bites, Luca massaged his hands together as well as place his elbows on the table. "So ... Where're you from?".

" Crystal City.".

" Right here in Crystal City. Good. Don't worry. I'm not going to ask anything else. Enjoy your dish. As well as slow down.".

" You're a youngster. But you chat like a grownup.".

" I'm thirteen," Luca replied. Is it too hot in below?".

The young boy wiped his forehead. "Not actually.".

" Okay, I need to do a number of things in the back, but I'll bring you a soft drink." Luca looked back at him again before going back to the kitchen, where he functioned quickly positioning containers of peppers, onions, garlic, as well as various other vegetables on a moving cart.

Minutes later on, Tony came via the door. "Lu, that's the kid out there asleep?".

" He's asleep?" Luca looked through the window of the door at the child. His head rested on his outstretched arm over the white and red checkered table linen. "He's from the neighborhood. My visitor.".

" Well, your visitor or otherwise," said his bro, "it does not look excellent to have someone oversleeping the dining establishment.".

" I'll care for it. And also simply maintain your mouth shut about it." "Why?".

" Since it's no one's organization." Luca walked into the dining area as well as broke a photo of the boy. He drank him. "Hey.".

The kid yawned and picked up his head. "I'm sorry. I can go.".

He showed him to the couch in his dad's workplace. "Pop is running errands. Go ahead.

He sat and looked around the workplace. Luca backed out of the room, and after that shut the door.

A few mins later, Luca examined him and also found him in a deep rest. However when he returned later on that mid-day with a plate of tiramisu, the child was gone. He 'd created 'thank you, buddy,' on a slip and left it on the sofa.

Luca sat holding the paper, asking yourself if he would certainly done the ideal thing. He 'd hoped he can obtain the kid house to his household without having to obtain the police entailed.

six

Luca looked up and also down the street. Luca kept looking over his shoulder to make sure the kid hadn't vanished. Luca led him to the bathroom, as well as the boy went in. Luca looked with the window of the door at the kid. Luca strolled into the eating area as well as broke a picture of the kid.

Anybody who invested any type of time with Luca wondered at how he appeared so much older than his years. Luca considered it a true blessing and also a curse. The dining establishment company was nowhere near what Luca desired for his life.

Lu, you friend is back! Tony shouted into the office the next day.

Luca went out front as well as located the boy sitting at a table near the door. Hey!

Uh, you re right here. I put on t also know your name. He waited, however the boy just stared at him.

All righty. You re anonymous. So, yeah, you re right here.

You simply stated that. Because you created on that note that you have something that belongs to me, I came back?.

Luca hit his forehead with the palm of his hand. Rest right here, he stated, directing at a chair. I ll go and obtain it.

Luca ran to the office, grabbed the little environment-friendly box from the desk cabinet, and also hurried back to the boy prior to he disappeared again. Luca rested throughout from him at the table.

Have you got it?.

I assume you re living on the street. He got the child s arm as he started to stand. Don t. Wait.

The kid unzipped his layer to his upper body, relaxed in his chair, and also kept an eye out the home window.

You re a youngster. Luca held his hand up toward the home window. You shouldn t be around like that.

You put on t know anything concerning me.

I I think I can aid you get home or obtain help. Luca held his breath, awaiting him to state something.

My name is Jared.

Thanks, Jared. I m Luca.

That s right, you do. It was on the note. You live below in Crystal City. Did you run away from house?.

Jared continued enjoying the park nearby.
You put on t wish to speak about you, hunh? I m like that as well, Luca claimed. Okay, so, how about this? If I tell you a secret about me, then will you answer my inquiry?.
Jared wrinkled his nose. Is this some sort of psychology trick? You find out about psychology?.
Who doesn t?.
Luca laughed. It s not.
Okay, after that. Go ahead, claimed Jared.
Luca decreased his voice. I wear t like it below. In Crystal City?.
No, collaborating with my family in this restaurant. My dad drives me nuts. He doesn t respect any one of my interests. I could be out doing various other points, yet I have to be right here constantly.
What other points?.
Luca thought for a minute. I don t recognize.
A minimum of you have a family members, Jared mumbled. You should be grateful. You re not out right here like me, alone and also not knowing where your next meal will certainly originate from, surviving on the he silenced and also touched the table.
Luca hoped Jared would certainly say extra, given that he finally obtained him speaking, yet he didn t. Your turn.
My turn? asked Jared.
Our contract. If I told you a trick, you were going to answer my concern.
I think I already did.
Luca s brows furrowed. I think so ... Well, tell me something else. Anything. What s on your mind? He expected information that would certainly result in locating Jared s family members.
You re going to believe it s childlike or dumb. No, I won t.
Jared was silent and also looked to be sizing Luca up. He talked slowly. Have you ever before...
Ever what? Claim it.
Have you ever before heard of a Christmas wonder? Luca s eyebrows increased. Yeah.
What concerning a birthday wish?.
His lips pursed. Naturally I have. Now you re joking around. Be significant. Jared leaned forward with his breast against the table. I am.

Check this out. The very first baby born on Christmas has the capacity to make a birthday desire that.
It s like a wish on steroids. Luca asked.
Doesn t matter. Yes, it does.
Jared cocked his head. Why?.
Luca leaned closer to him. Since my mama was the only person I ever heard reference it.
Jared s eyes lightened up. Truly?.
It s so weird that you know about it. I believed she made it up. Did you have a wish like that?.
No, Jared replied. Do I look like I made some big desire? If my wishes became a reality, parents wouldn t die, as well as individuals wouldn t be homeless. He stood.
Jared!.
Consumers examined at them.
Take a seat, Luca murmured. Did I miss out on something? What s wrong?.
Jared evaluated his shoulder toward Luca s papa. Your father isn t so negative. I wager if you speak to him about the kind of things you like to do, he ll take rate of interest.
Luca trembled his head. He only cares concerning the restaurant.
You believe so? Yep.
Luca scratched his chin. I m not, Jared firmly insisted.
Luca watched him. He maintained checking out the clock on the wall. Do you have someplace to be?.
Yes, I d better go. See ya, Jared replied and also hurried out.
Luca encountered the kitchen area and also ordered his layer. Tony, cover for me.
Tony sought out from the sink, where he was washing meals. Why? Stop attempting to be a hero.
I m not. Pop, I ll be right back, Luca screamed.
He rushed outside, after that looked both ways down the road for Jared. He detected the young boy s coat between buyers in the next block. The sunlight was establishing, creating his grey coat to mix into the sundown. Luca followed him, but not as well close. When he slowed, Luca approached him. Jared leaned forward, speaking to somebody.

Jared?.
His head jerked up. What are you doing? Did you follow me? That were you talking to?.
Jared spun about. You made her leave. She s gone once more. His entire countenance changed, as if he would certainly rupture right into rips.
Hey man, cool down. I only tried to find you because you neglected this, Luca claimed as he held up his hand, exposing the box he d placed the locket inside of.
Jared took it from him. I ve obtained ta go.
Jared frowned. You believe I stole it? I spent for it. I was only asking.
Jared left without another word, seemingly mad. Luca followed him.
Where are you going?.
To discover my sis.
You have a sister? Let me assist you discover her.
You can t. Jared stopped. You re going to maintain following me, aren t you?.
The thought had crossed my mind, Luca replied. So where do we. look?.
Actually?.
Yep?.
Jared frowned. Don t you need to go make a pizza? Nope.
Penalty.

seven

Luca adhered to Jared to McKinney Park. They walked over the snow-covered lawn, around the mini train youngsters were boarding as Walking in a Winter months Wonderland played from its speakers, to the rock fountain of a mommy as well as youngster at the center of the park.

She s right here? asked Luca, browsing.

She will be, Jared replied. I simply need to be right here when she comes.

That might be any time of day. Luca massaged his head as Jared began to leave. Wait, where are you going?.

I have to keep strolling. I put on t recognize what side of the park she ll get to.

Luca complied with carefully, browsing, but not recognizing that he was seeking. After two hours, he assumed he would certainly freeze to death.

Why wear t you come home with me, as well as we ll try once again tomorrow?

I wear t believe so.

Look, it s much better than resting wherever it is you sleep. My pop won't mind. I need to make one quit first. He grabbed Jared s shoulders. Come on, he said happily. You know you wish to.

Jared didn t respond, however he complied with Luca to a shop a couple of blocks away.

Vigo, Luca shouted from the entry. The only olive oil we use, he murmured to Jared as they strolled past the racks of veggie oils in the adjacent space.

Vigo looked up from the till at the front of the next area. Luca, hi ...

Whoa, you understand just family members is permitted back below. He he s my relative.

He s black. That s right, I am, claimed Jared with a smirk.

Luca positioned his arm over Jared s shoulders. We're a multicultural family member. Vigo chose a box up and also placed it in Luca s arms. We require more of that. He grinned at Jared. Invite to the family. And consume something, would ya. You're going to make individuals assume we deprive you.

Will certainly do, sir, stated Jared. I like him, said Vigo. It s going to be a cold one tonight.

They exited the store as well as Luca counted on Jared. You have a means with individuals.

Not all individuals. Do we require to catch a bus or something?

Nope. We're not far from my house, claimed Luca. You live midtown?

Sure do. It's midway in between both of our dining establishment locations.

Luca moved the box against his hip. And also look, if Maria asks that you are, you re a trainee at Fletcher.

That s Maria? Jared asked. Did she inform you about the Christmas wonder desire?

No, that was my birth parent. Maria is my stepmom. She s great. If she asks, you were skipped up a quality 2 qualities, as well as we fulfilled in chess. club.

Jared tilted his head. Did you just make all of that up? Yeah, and whatever you do, do not drink her eggnog. The temperature level was dropping outdoors, so they strolled quickly. Luca maintained reversing, watching Jared. His speed slowed down, as well as he coughed hard.

Hey, are you okay? Luca asked. Jared nodded.

I assume we have some throat lozenges at the house. Thanks, stated Jared.

That home right there, said Luca, pointing with his joint.

Jared followed him across the street and up the stairways. The front door opened up as quickly as they came close to.

Hey Maria, Luca stated. Here s package of olive oil from Vigo, and also I have a buddy with me. She nodded as well as shut the door behind them. I can see that. Are you mosting likely to present us?.

He established package unemployed beside the door. This is Jared, he claimed as he took off his headscarf and hat and also stuck them in his pockets.

Hey there Jared. Just how do you recognize each other?.

I most likely to Fletcher. I missed a quality two grades, as well as we fulfilled in chess club, Jared rattled off. Luca shut his eyes and shook his head.

Well, I think that describes it, Maria said with a chuckle. Luca mosted likely to the stairs and also gestured to Jared. Show up below. Jared grinned at Maria and also followed Luca.

They went to his room, and Luca handed him a bag of lemon lozenges from his workdesk drawer.

Thanks. Good room. Jared popped a lozenge into his mouth.

Luca got an armful of clothes from his chair as well as tossed them on the floor of his storage room.

He stated as he chose up a remote as well as flipped via TV networks. There s absolutely nothing on tv however Christmas flicks.

Jared sat in the chair, still holding the lozenges. Do I look 5 years of ages to you? Any ages watch traditional holiday movies. You intend to attempt something? Like what?

A video game. Tony and I do it constantly. You select which character you intend to be, reject the quantity, as well as we ll do their voices.

Jared looked entertained. Okay. I m Snoopy. I ll be Charlie.

Jared laid on the flooring on his back.

You're really getting into character, Luca claimed with a laugh and utilized the remote to deny the tv. They saw Charlie Brown walk outside of his house. I m outside due to the fact that my home scents like farts, said Luca.

What do you desire me to do regarding it? Jared asked, being Snoopy laying on top of his doghouse.

Luca asked. He was taken, as well as it s all my mistake. It s always your mistake.

No, it s not, Jared stated, his voice rising. What occurred, Snoopy?.

This is dumb.

Luca held up a Nerf Dart Blaster. Hurry and tell me, before I fire your huge nose with a dart.

Jared rolled over. I said this is foolish! I don t want to play this video game anymore.

Oh, I assumed you were still in character. No worry. Luca switched the channel to a different movie. Titanic?.

Jared shrugged.

The boys fell asleep on the flooring. Luca awoke and also went downstairs with his laptop. He rested at the dining-room table and Googled Xmas miracle wish.

His father strolled in, not discovering him, and went over to the Xmas tree. He stood there a minute.

Pop what are you doing? Luca asked. Are you ready to begin detaching tiny items of the covering paper, trying to see what the gifts are once more?.

No. His daddy sighed. Annually I remember this crazy thing your mommy utilized to claim about Xmas miracles.

What regarding it?

It's that time of year. Something huge is mosting likely to take place. It constantly does. Actually?

His father rubbed his eyes. Pop, are you sobbing?

No. He smelled. I put on t cry. What are you doing up? It's late. Are you laying some game?

Jared was silent and looked to be sizing Luca up. Jared looked over his shoulder towards Luca s dad. Luca maintained transforming back, seeing Jared. Luca went to the stairs and gestured to Jared. Jared grinned at Maria and complied with Luca.

"No, Pop. I'm doing research."

He walked up behind Luca's chair, considering the laptop screen. "This has to do with that kid, isn't it?"

" Yeah. He said his mommy passed."

" Oh boy. That's a hard one to deal with," his dad said as he pulled up a chair.

Luca, shocked, ran over. His father pointed at the screen.

" The Google? "I know a point or 2.

" Google that as well as click on information."

Luca glanced over at his daddy as he aimed at a post. Jared was right.

His dad wanted what he did. Luca reviewed the headings. "Look, a lady had a cardiac arrest in 2014.

There's no mention of kids."

" Seek out the funeral service documents," his dad suggested. "Also a funeral program will certainly state 'made it through by' or something to that effect."

" Wait. It's right here," claimed Luca. Jared's not making it up.

A siren blasted on the road, and also he and also his dad looked toward the picture window.

Luca stood. Lights flashed beyond their house. "That called the cops? Where's Tony?"

Footprints bounded down the stairways. "Jared, wait!" Luca called out.

It was as well late. Jared bolted outdoors. The back storm door knocked losed behind him.

eight

Jared ran till he no longer listened to alarms. He stopped, leaning beside a structure, attempting to capture his breath.

A guy's sharp voice originated from behind him. "Hey, what are you doing back there?"

Jared rejected the street.

The law enforcement officer pursued him. "Hey, stop!"

He ran as well as transformed the edge throughout the street, via web traffic with horns warning and headlights blinking in his eyes. Jared allowed out a small yelp, then leapt up on a parked cars and truck and also moved across the hood.

His rate slowed down as he ran behind the filling bay of a house improvement shop, seeing to it to remain in the darkness. On the other side of the store, he quit to capture his breath, particular he 'd shed the officer.

Hands appeared of no place and grabbed Jared, lifting him up. Jared's feet pedaled airborne.

The policeman put him down.

" Let me go," Jared yelled as he tried to release his arm from the officer's understanding.

" Cool down. I'm mosting likely to let you go. Do not run. Do you hear me?" The police officer pointed a finger at him.

" Okay! I hear you!"

" What are you doing out below right now of evening?" "Are you going to detain me?"

" Arrest you?" The police officer damaged his head. "More like take you home.

Where do you live?"

" 170 Dumpster Street," Jared claimed, being ironical.

The officer's eyes expanded. "You're including me." He drew him along by the shoulder of his coat.

" No, wait!"

Jared was dragged down an additional block as well as up the stairways of a church. The policeman opened the door as well as pressed Jared inside.

" Why do you have tricks to a church? I assumed you were a law enforcement agent," he claimed, looking into the police officer's attire as well as badge.

" I am, as well as I'm also a priest. Begin," he claimed, walking down the facility aisle, between church benches. He turned past a display screen of Xmas trees with little white lights.

Jared stopped, drinking his head. "I'm not coming back there. What's back there?"

The male stepped back forward with his hands on his hips. "Oh, currently you're afraid. You weren't afraid on the roads, but you hesitate in a church? Astounding."

Jared looked behind him at the doors, observing the policeman didn't secure them in. He could leave if he wanted. He supported, checked out the stained-glass windows, and after that adhered to the officer.

A light shone from a room down the hall. He strolled to the entryway and saw the policeman open a small fridge and set a sandwich as well as beverage on

his workdesk. "I'm not being available in there."

" You will if you want to consume," the guy replied. "However not like that. Go following door and clean your face as well as hands. Come back and also eat the lunch my wife fastidiously prepared that I didn't eat today. I'm just saying. It'll assist me out. I won't have to exist as well as inform her I ate it."

" You're in a church. You can't exist."

" Oops. I neglected," the pastor stated with a smile.

Jared went to the bathroom. He would certainly forgotten what he looked like. His eyes looked older, as if he would certainly matured ten years.
He cleaned his face and hands as well as stood there for a minute. Short hissing noises came from him.
" Are you alright in there, or did you choose to leap out of the home window?" asked the policeman from outside the door.
Jared turned the water off as well as browsed him as the door opened. "I ruined your washroom, I'm sorry." He stooped on the flooring, cleaning up the wet areas with a paper towel.
The officer patted Jared's shoulder. Come and consume."
Jared followed the police officer back to his workdesk. He 'd added an apple to the sandwich as well as drink.
The officer sat as well as pointed at the sandwich. "It's some kind of luncheon meat, gouda cheese and also avocado. Are you adverse anything?"
Jared shook his head. Why really did not you consume it?
" No. It's nothing like that I had pizza, but she doesn't want me eating that. He wiggled his eyebrows and held a finger to his lips. "Shh, do not tell my spouse.
" What, is she coming here or something?"
" She may. She resembles a ghost and appears out of no place."
Jared took a tiny bite of the sandwich and also ate, then he took a much larger bite and also ate quicker. His jaws chomped like a beaver.
" Hey, slow down. I think it tastes far better than I thought. Perhaps I should've eaten it. Here, drink," he stated, handing Jared the juice. "Why were you out currently of evening?"
Jared swallowed his mouthful of food. "I'm looking for my sis." "She's missing?"
" Maybe. Are you going to transform me in? I'm simply going to run away

once again due to the fact that if you do. As well as I'll keep running up until I locate her. My mommy wouldn't like
--".
" Where is your mother?".
Jared averted from him. "Gone.".
The police officer researched Jared as he pushed the sandwich away as well as consumed the juice. "Do you rely on wonders?".
" Are you ready to rattle off a list of reasons that I should have the Xmas spirit or count on Christmas wonders?" Jared put the bottle on the desk. "Why are you looking at me like that?".
The policeman leaned closer to Jared. "Some of the greatest wonders take area during Xmas.".
" Whatever.".
The policeman opened his desk cabinet. Look at this book.
" Let me think, these are all individuals you know, right?".
The pastor pointed at the open page. "These kids.
He turned the web page and also pointed once again. "Households needing cash to maintain their houses as well as somebody true blessing them, or requiring food and individuals showing up with it. Long-lost household members coming house.".
Jared searched for at him. "If you go on believing, the dream that you wish will come to life.".
The officer set down the publication. Jared picked up the various other half of the sandwich.
my young boys I know that quote or that I even watched the flick. I needed to because of my sister.".
"Mikey may. He appears when there's food about.".
The officer giggled, realizing Jared duplicated the joke he 'd made regarding

his spouse a moment earlier. "You're amusing.".

Jared took an additional bite of the sandwich as well as talked with his mouth full. He looked right into the policeman's eyes. "I only have till Christmas.".

The policeman slanted his head. "What does that suggest?" "I simply have to discover her.".

"Go where? To the authorities terminal?".

" No. Someplace even worse.".

" Honey, I'm home," the police officer called as they entered his home.

His partner came around the edge, her arms folded up over her breast. "This is a little as well late in the evening for you to come in all cheery-jolly, Mister! She quieted, seeing Jared.

Her face softened as she neared him, wearing her bathrobe and slippers, her hair in a messy bun. She stopped a couple of feet from him. "Okay, I don't recognize whose child you are, yet you are going directly to the shower.".

Jared's mouth dropped open. "However--".

She pointed to the stairs. She transformed to her hubby. Discover him something to wear.".

The police officer and also Jared started to climb the stairways. "See, worse than the authorities," the policeman murmured.

He loved that regarding his partner. She didn't care that the kid was, she was going to deal with him.

An hour later on, clean, putting on one of the policeman's tees and also his spouse's boxers for shorts, Jared emerged from the restroom and also walked downstairs.

He transformed, listening to the front door open. The police officer's better half walked in with bags as well as established them on the dining room table.

" Where have you been?" asked her other half.

" One of the three stores in the city that's open all evening. It was a madhouse out there, with all the final Christmas shoppers.".

" After that why did you head out? It couldn't wait till tomorrow?" the officer asked.

" I couldn't perhaps allow him place those clothes back on, and they are not going in our washer. "Are you using my boxers? I'm Erica, by the method," she claimed as she pulled the items out of the bags.

He walked over as well as looked at the coats and also jeans she put on the table.

" You got him a hideous sweatshirt?" "What's wrong with it?".

" It's an ugly Xmas coat. He's not going to wish to wear that." The policeman frowned. "That's why our nephews as well as nieces choose we give them cash for Xmas, as a result of you and also these awful sweatshirts.".

" It's Christmas, and we're all using them this year.".

Jared practically grinned, paying attention to them. "These are nice, yet I can't take them. I need to go back out.".

" Not this evening, you don't," stated Erica. "I have to search for my sibling.".

" Exactly how regarding we aid you look for her tomorrow?" asked Policeman Ken. Jared rubbed his arm nervously. "You're not mosting likely to transform me in to the.

Department of Kid as well as Households?".

Ken touched the counter top. "Allow's simply wait on that a minute." Jared smiled.

" We have an extra bed room. Jared looked at Ken.

Ken held a finger to his

lips. "Yes, pizza."

"Oh wait. I have a toothbrush for you, too."

Later, after he'd brushed his teeth, Jared followed Ken and Erica to the guest room and allowed them to tuck him in. He watched them as they held hands, closed their eyes, and said a prayer for him. Then he laid in the dark, staring at the tiny globe, barely giving off enough light to be called a night light.

"So who is our visitor?" asked
Erica.

Ken gave her a sad look. "He's a runaway."

"But he says he's looking for his sister. Is she younger or

older?" "I don't know. She's still out there, I guess."

Erica put a hand above her heart. "He's only, like, ten, I think. How long do you think he's been on the streets?"

"I don't know, but by the sound of things, they catch him, and he runs again."

"Maybe she's been gone a while, then. If she's even

alive." Ken held up a hand. "Shh . . . Listen."

They put their ears to the wall.

Erica looked at her husband. "Who is he talking

to?" "Is he praying?" Ken asked.

"That's not praying," said Erica. "He's carrying on a conversation."

"Where have you been, Snicker?"

"Tell me a story," she said as she snuggled in beside him. She smelled of bubble gum and he wondered where she'd gotten it. Maybe someone had been kind to her too. For once, they were falling asleep without their bellies growling and without the cold air burning their cheeks. They didn't even have to stuff their coats with all the paper or clothes they could find for warmth.

Jared thought for a moment, then started his story. "There once was a little girl who had magical wishes because she was the first child born on Christmas day. She received one miracle wish a year that would come true."

"What would you wish for, Brother?" asked Snicker with a yawn.

"I don't know," Jared said as he held her, and his eyes began to close. "Don't forget about the park, Snicker," he whispered.

"Never," she said and fell asleep.

Nine

Jared awoke and stared at the nightstand beside him. He'd almost forgotten where he was. He pushed the comforter back and climbed out of bed, pulling up the oversized socks his feet didn't quite fill, and went to the door. There wasn't a sound anywhere in the house.

The stairs were right next to his room. He snuck downstairs and put on the jeans and two of the sweaters Erica had purchased. His coat hung on a coat rack near the front door. He reached in the pocket for a throat lozenge and walked through the house, looking for a paper and pen to write on.

One of the walls in the kitchen was painted with chalkboard paint. He took one of the pieces of chalk and wrote Ken and Erica a note.

When they awoke, Jared was gone. They watched everything he'd done on their home camera system.

Erica glanced at her husband. "He left us a thank you note."

Ken sat with his elbows on his desk, watching the video, and breathed into his clasped hands. "Yeah, he's a good kid."

"Where do you think he went?" asked Erica.

"I don't know. He hasn't been gone that long. It shouldn't be too hard to find him. I'll put out a—Wait, where's my phone? Did he take my phone?"

Erica looked under the bags on the table. "Do you know what else he took?"

"What?"

"The ugly sweater."

Ken rubbed his forehead. "Erica, who cares about a sweater? I need my phone."

"You're a police officer. Track it."

She noticed the box of cereal open on the counter, the banana peel on the table, and wrinkled her nose at what looked to be vomit in the trash can.

"And you need to hurry. I think he's sick."

Officer Ken walked downtown, looking everywhere for Jared. His wife drove, checking side streets and alleys. He came across a teen with a long shag haircut and bangs hanging over his eyes, stopping pedestrians and showing them his phone.

"Excuse me, Ma'am," the teen said to a woman who had stopped to look. "Have you seen this kid? I think he's in danger."

"No. I'm sorry. I haven't," she replied.

"What about you, sir?" he said to a man who ignored him and kept walking. "You don't have to be rude. It's Christmas. You're going on the naughty list!" he yelled after him.

Officer Ken walked over to him. "Hey, what's your name,

kid?" "Uh, Jeff."

"Jeff, huh? You don't look like a Jeff to me. Let's try that again. What's your real name?"

The boy swallowed.

"Luca." "What have you

got there?"

Luca looked around and put his phone in his pocket.

Officer Ken held out his hand. "It's too late for that, kid. Let me see it."

Luca showed him the photo.

"You know Jared?"

Luca's brows rose. "How do you—Oh, you're looking to take him away or something."

"No. I'm looking to help him. When was the last time you saw him?" Ken asked.

"I don't know. When was the last time you saw him?"

"Look, this is no time for games. I think he's ill. I need to find him."

"I got that idea too. But I don't know where he is. I only know he's looking for his sister," said Luca. "I was going to go to the apartment building he used to live in next and ask around."

Ken raised his brows. "What

building?" "Oops. Did I mention a

building?" "Yes, you did."

Luca didn't respond.

"Unless you would prefer to get arrested . . ." Officer Ken said while removing his handcuffs.

Luca backed away from him. "Webster Place. But it was my idea, so I'm going too."

"Let's go, then." Ken motioned for Luca to join him.

"Are you going to read me my rights?"

"I'm not arresting you."

"I just want to see what it's like. You know, get the full experience."

"Kid, where are your parents?"

"Man, I'm riding in an actual police car. Cool," said Luca, looking back at the plexiglass separating the back seat from the front.

Ken chuckled. "Well, that's not the reaction I'm used

to." "You mean from criminals?"

"Yes. And you wouldn't be here if your father hadn't said it was okay. Now, back to Jared. Tell me everything you know."

"What is all that stuff on your belt?" Luca pointed at Ken's waist. "Tasers or something? Do all police cruisers have a full-on office? Can I use your computer?"

"Don't touch anything. Hands in your lap and keep them there," Officer Ken said as he glanced at his side mirror and began to pull out of the parking space. "Again, tell me what you know about Jared."

There was a tap on the window and Ken slammed on the breaks. Luca's eyes widened. "Pop?"

"Are you going to open the door for me, or should I ride on the hood?" his father shouted from the street.

"What are you doing?" asked Luca.

His father gave him an exasperated look. "I told you I was coming with you."

"I thought you were joking."

"I should let my son get hauled off to jail or something? Are you kidding me?"

Officer Ken opened the door of the back seat. Luca's father looked inside. "I can't fit back there."

"Pop, I'm riding in front," Luca told him. "I have to show him the way."

"No, you don't," said Officer Ken. "Can you guys hurry up and work this out?"

"I'm getting in," said Luca's father.

"I can't believe this," Officer Ken muttered.

"What is this, plastic?" Luca's father asked from the backseat. "This is the most uncomfortable thing I've ever felt. I'm packed in here like a sardine!"

"Pop, just—"

"Would you two, stop?" Officer Ken exclaimed. He pulled the car into the street.

They fell silent, listening to the wipers work to clear the windshield of the light snow.

"Something is going to happen if Jared doesn't find his sister by Christmas, and he's serious about it," said Luca. "Like it's a mission he has to complete. He looks for her every day at the park."

"Which park?" Officer Ken asked.

"Downtown. McKinney Park. Across from our restaurant. He believes in a —in a—" Luca was reluctant to say it aloud. "A Christmas miracle."

Officer Ken grinned. "Good."

"Good?" Luca twisted to look at him. "You mean you believe too? Why is that good, though?"

"I believe too," his father said from the backseat.

Officer Ken gave Luca a serious look. "Because it means he still has hope."

"I guess. Oh, I caught him talking to someone that wasn't there—That's it! That's Webster Place, right there." Luca pointed at the apartment building just ahead.

Officer Ken stopped the car alongside two vehicles parked against the curb in front of the building.

"That's so cool how you can just block traffic like that, because you're the popo," said Luca.

Officer Ken frowned. "Don't call me that."

"Would someone let me out of here!" Luca's father yelled.

They walked up to the front doors of the brick building. "So what was your plan?" asked Luca's father.

Officer Ken looked over his shoulder at Luca. "I didn't really have a plan," said Luca.

"No, plan? Are you kidding me?" His father rubbed his forehead. "Pop, I'm still figuring things out."

Officer Ken shook his head. "Well, while you're figuring it out, what did Jared—"

"Jared? The little boy, Jared?" asked a woman passing to enter the building.

"Yes, do you know him? I'm Pastor Ken."

Luca's head jerked toward him, shocked. "Pop, did you hear that? He's a pastor."

"I heard," his father replied.

"Mrs. Hollis," she said, shaking his hand. "I knew his mother." "Can we talk somewhere?" Ken asked her.

The four of them walked to the coffee shop up the street and sat in one of the booths. Ken called Erica, and a few minutes later, she joined them.

Once everyone was settled with hot drinks, Mrs. Hollis stirred her coffee. "I was there when Jared found his mother. That poor child. It was horrible. I never want to see someone in that kind of pain again."

"What happened after that?" asked Officer Ken. "He went into foster care."

"And his sister?"

"I don't know." Mrs. Hollis teared up. "I thought they both did. I didn't hear anything more after that."

"No one kept up with the case?" Erica asked.

Mrs. Hollis shook her head sadly. "No. They had no family."

"Wow. Okay." Ken exchanged a worried glance with his

wife.

"Hey, check it out," said Luca, pointing at the television mounted in the corner of the room near the ceiling.

Everyone turned to the screen.

"There's a blizzard heading this way?" asked Erica.

Officer Ken stood. "I've got to go. Thank you, Mrs. Hollis. Please, give us a call if you think of anything else that might help us find Jared, or if you hear from him."

"There is something else." Mrs. Hollis said, raising a finger. "I know that Jared talks about finding his sister, but there was a little girl that passed about two weeks after his mother. Lately, I've been wondering if it was her. I'm sure you can look into it."

"Mrs. Hollis, how did his mother die?" asked Erica.

"She had a weak heart. So did his sister."

ten

"Mikey, it's me," Jared said into Officer Ken's

phone. "Jared? Is this your new cell?"

"No, I borrowed it. What are you doing?"

"What am I usually doing?" Mikey replied. "Watching Fortnite on YouTube."

"Forget that," Jared said. "You need to check out this guy, Spencer, playing Mario and Sonic. He's good."

"Dude, no one is thinking about those retro

games." "Yes, they are. That's why they're on

YouTube." Mikey's dad said something in the

background. "Huh?" Mikey replied to him.

"Okay, I will." "Your dad sounds like Vin

Diesel."

"You've said that like a thousand times." Mikey paused. "Hey, you flying the coop?"

"Yeah."

"I got you. It'll be

open." "Thanks man."

Jared tossed the phone in a trash can and hurried to Mikey's house.

Only a small person could fit inside Mikey's basement window. It opened toward the driveway, but only halfway. Jared climbed in feet first, lowered himself onto the washing machine, and hopped off it. Behind the laundry room was the furnace room, where he hid whenever Mikey helped him out.

Mikey had already put a pillow, sleeping bag, Lunchable, and bottled water in there for him. Mikey didn't usually join him if his parents were home. They would know something was up, because he didn't usually go to the basement unless they sent him down to get something like tools or clothes from the dryer.

It was snowing hard outside, and the wind was howling. Jared took off his boots, laid on top of the sleeping bag, and slept straight through the day— only waking for a few sips of water.

The next morning, he awoke to the smell of bacon and eggs. He loved Mikey's mom's chilaquiles. He was glad she didn't make that, because for the first time in maybe his whole life, he had no appetite.

Soft holiday music played.

"It's Christmas morning," he said as he sat up and leaned back against the cinder block wall. His breathing was shallow, and though he wore layers and it was a warm house, he had chills.

There were loud footsteps overhead. He stood and stumbled into the wall. Then he grabbed hold of the door frame and steadied himself. He went to the bottom of the stairs and listened to the conversation taking place in the kitchen.

"¡Qué va! Mikey, are you helping him?" asked his mother with a Spanish accent.

"No."

"Don't you lie," said his Vin Diesel-dad.

"I only give him some of my allowance

sometimes." "What's wrong with you?" his mom

asked.

"Nothing. You always tell me to do what's right. That was right."

"Giving a runaway your money is not right. That doesn't really help him," said his dad.

"I'm helping him find his sister."

"Sister, huh? Have you seen this sister before?" asked another male voice.

"Yeah," Mikey replied, sounding scared.

"You have?" the man

pressed. "Yeah. But not

recently."

His mom sounded frustrated. "More of what we keep hearing—a sister who doesn't exist."

Jared bit his lip.

"You don't know that," said a voice he recognized. "You've seen the record we found—the obituary."

Jared's head lowered. He braced himself against the banister and climbed up the stairs. Every few seconds, his lungs felt like they were being squeezed and released. He pushed the basement door open.

Vin Diesel-dad almost jumped up on the stove. His mom grabbed the broom.

Mikey's eyes were as wide as everyone else's seeing him standing there. As if he didn't know Jared was in the house.

"Mikey . . ." said his dad, holding his chest.

"Pastor-Officer Ken, my sister isn't dead," said Jared.

He looked into his eyes. "I really want to help you, Jared. I really do." "You said you believe in miracles."

"I do." Ken nodded.

Jared gave him a pleading look. "Then you have to believe me."

"How can I believe you?"

"I can show you."

eleven

"Yes, we're on the way there now. I'll see you there," Officer Ken said and disconnected the call.

"I'm just saying. This is a big mistake," his partner complained. "Stop."

"Just wait. You'll see. There won't be any—" "Stop!"

His partner quieted and shifted in his seat. "You're awfully testy for a Christmas morning," he mumbled.

Officer Ken drove in silence the rest of the way. The roads had a fresh covering of snow and hadn't been driven over. He parked the car.

"Wait here, Murphy." he told his partner. "Your negativity doesn't help anything."

"Yeah, right." Murphy got out of the car and joined his side. "I wouldn't miss this for the world."

Officer Ken got out of the car and let Jared out of the backseat. Jared held to the door for a moment.

"Hey, are you okay?" Ken asked him.

Jared nodded as Officer Ken's wife parked behind the patrol car with Mrs. Hollis beside her.

"Jared, you can stay here," Officer Ken said. "I can search for her." "No," Jared shook his head. "I have to show you."

Mikey and his parents pulled up. Luca, Tony, and their father stood at the Main Street entrance of the park.

"I feel like a spaceship is going to land in front of us or something," said Luca.

Officer Ken turned toward him. "Where is she, Jared? Now is your chance —your last chance."

Jared hugged his elbows. "I don't know exactly.""Listen, you said she's here, and despite all the evidence, I'm trying to believe—to believe—"

"In a Christmas miracle?" Jared asked in almost a whisper. Officer Ken nodded. Jared turned and walked into the park. Everyone followed him to the center and stood in front of the statue of a mother and child.

"If she's here, what will she be doing?" asked

Tony. "Looking for me," said Jared.

Tony shook his head. "I can't."

His father pointed at him. "You! Shut it!"

Officer Ken scanned the area. "We can see most of the park from here. Maybe we should split up and look around."

"Yes, let's do that," said Erica, throwing Tony an irritated

look. "Do you believe him?" Mikey's father asked Luca's

father.

"If I didn't, I wouldn't be here." He rubbed Luca's shoulders. "I trust what my son believes. After hearing the whole story, I think I want it to be true for him."

Officer Ken went in one direction. Mikey's family in another.

"I guess we should go this way," Luca said, leading his family away.

Erica, Mrs. Hollis, and Officer Murphy stayed with Jared, watching him closely as he walked. His breathing became increasingly heavier, and the front of his hat dampened from his sweating.

He stopped walking and brushed snow from a bench. "I need to sit for a minute."

"Jared, sweetie, we don't see anything. I think we need to get you to a doctor," said Mrs. Hollis.

"No. I have to wait." Tears filled his eyes. "I have to. It's my last chance. I have to—"

Erica turned sharply, looking around the park. "What was that? Did you hear that?"

Jared sat erect.

A high-pitched, faint scream came from not far

off. Officer Murphy's mouth dropped. "It's a

cat." "No, it's not. Snicker!" Jared screamed.

"Jared, that could be anyone," said Mrs. Hollis.

"It's not anyone." Jared stood, walked quickly away from them, and then began to run.

"Hey, wait. Slow down!" called Erica, rushing after him.

"Snicker!" he screamed as he ran as fast as he could. He yelled her name over and over. Not like a person calling out to someone, but like a person wailing in pain.

The others heard it too and came running.

Jared stopped, looked around, and waited. He heard the scream again and darted to the left. He stumbled back a little and looked like he was about to lean backward.

Mikey ran forward and grabbed him, throwing Jared's arm over his shoulder, and his arm around Jared's waist. "Come on, man. You're not giving up now. I'm the only one who ever believed you, get those legs moving. I've got you. I may not be fast, but I'm strong."

They ran together, with Mikey almost dragging Jared.

A little girl, wearing a red coat and white hat with a pom on top and two poms hanging from her white mittens, stood on top of a snow-covered bench.

Two adults were nearing her with their arms outstretched as if trying to get her to quiet down.

"Snicker!" Jared screamed again. "I'm

here!" Mike let go of him, and he slumped

forward.

Everyone stopped running and watched him. Jared's steps were as if in slow motion. He stopped.

Officer Ken bolted to him. "No, no, no!" he exclaimed as Jared's eyes rolled back and he collapsed.

twelve

Beep. Beep.

Jared heard the sound every few seconds.

"Brother," a tiny voice said over and over. "Brother, please wake up."

Jared slowly opened his eyes. "Snicker," he tried to say. But his mouth was so dry he choked.

Officer Ken's voice floated over him. "Get him some ice chips."

Snicker climbed up on the bed and hugged his neck. "I found you. I remembered the park. Just like you said. Just like you told me every night."

The two adults behind her looked at each other. "Every night?" Jared didn't recognize them.

"I can't get over this. How did they not tell us she had a brother when we adopted her?" said the man.

"How did you find him?" Officer Ken asked.

"We didn't," said the woman. "She did. It was her birthday wish."

"Today is her birthday?"

"Yes."

Jared sucked on an ice chip from the cup Officer Ken held to his mouth. He slowly lifted his hand and pulled one of Snicker's pigtails.

"Who blew out your hair? Mom liked it natural."

"It was only the one time . . ." the woman's voice trailed off as her husband pulled her back and silenced her.

"I never stopped looking for you." A tear fell from Jared's eye. Snicker hugged him again.

"Your mother would be so proud of you," said Mrs. Hollis from the door.

The man spoke again. "Siobhan didn't want to open gifts. She wanted to go to a park, but not just any park. We argued against it because of the snow. But she demanded and screamed and threw the worst tantrum we'd ever seen from her. It had to be today. She screamed when she saw the park and wouldn't stop screaming."

"We should let him rest," said his

wife. "No, I won't go," Snicker cried.

"Don't you worry, honey.," the woman said soothingly. "We will never let you two be separated again."

Officer Ken held Jared's hand and smiled down at him. He wagged a finger. "I tell you, those Christmas miracles . . ."

Three weeks later . . .

Jared and Snicker sat on the floor in front of a six-foot Christmas tree with gifts of all shapes and sizes beneath it. A fireplace to the left warmed them. An almost collapsed gingerbread house that Snicker had decorated with too many gumdrops sat on the coffee table behind them with mugs of eggnog and assorted desserts. Christmas images expanded in and out on the wall mounted television, accompanied by a jazz rendition of "Silent Night".

Their new godparents, Ken and Erica, sat with their new parents, the Clincys. Luca and his father, Mikey, and Mrs. Hollis were also there for the late Christmas celebration.

"I have something for you," Jared said to his sister. He placed the necklace he had gotten for his mother over Snicker's head.

Snicker smiled from ear to ear. She reached under the tree and handed him a small flat gift that could have been just gift wrap. By the looks of it, she had wrapped it herself. Jared carefully peeled off the tape and pulled back the red paper, revealing a small white envelope.

The note inside read, 'Snicker's wish'. He unfolded the paper and grinned at Snicker's handwriting,

To find my brother on Christmas.

You see, Jared had to believe that his sister loved him so much that there was only one thing she would have wished for on her miracle birthday—the only way they would find each other. And as you've already figured out, Snicker was never with Jared, although she heard him every night in her dreams telling her to remember the park. I believe a certain Christmas angel had something to do with that.

How did they get separated in the first place? Well, the very first foster home they were sent to had an abusive foster parent. But the man was only that way with the older kids. Jared ran away. In the short time he was gone, to cover up what he'd done, the man changed the paperwork to show Snicker was an only child. Shortly after, a couple, originally wanting to adopt an African American infant, fell in love with Snicker.

When Jared was recovered, he found that Snicker was gone. He was distraught and vowed to find her. Imagining Snicker was with him was his way of dealing with leaving her and staying strong until he found her again.

We only interfered a little, pushing him in her direction, because he had faith. Now Pastor Ken has another miracle to add to his book—a miracle he witnessed and was a part of. This miracle opened the eyes of many and caused them to have renewed hope.

Mission completed. Our work is done.

If you wonder where we are, look up at the stars during Christmas. If you see two of them moving, it's probably us, making things happen, or looking after Snicker's wish.

www.ingramcontent.com/pod-product-compliance
Lightning Source LLC
LaVergne TN
LVHW040912150826
845672LV00007B/2014
* 9 7 9 8 7 5 7 4 8 0 2 7 5 *